# FIRST GRADE US HISTORY THE FIRST PRESIDENT

Speedy Publishing LLC
40 E. Main St. #1156
Newark, DE 19711
www.speedypublishing.com

George Washington was
the first President of the
United States.

George
Washington
grew up in
Colonial Virginia.
His father, a
landowner and
planter

On January 6,
1759, Washington
married
the wealthy
widow Martha
Dandridge Custis.

George Washington served two terms as the first U.S. president, from 1789 to 1797.

He was the
only president
unanimously
elected. Meaning
all of the state
representatives
voted for him.

George Washington is known for leading the Continental Army in victory over the British in the American Revolution.

George Washington was one of the Founding Fathers of the United States. During his lifetime he was called the "father of his country".

He never served as president in Washington D.C., the capital that was named for him.